P9-EDU-427

TRAVELS
IN
NORTH AMERICA:

PARTICULARLY IN

THE PROVINCES OF UPPER & LOWER CANADA, AND NEW BRUNSWICK,

AND IN

THE STATES OF MAINE, MASSACHUSETS, AND NEW-YORK:

CONTAINING

A Variety of Interesting Adventures and Disasters, which the Author encountered in his Journey among the Americans, Dutch, French, and Indians.

ALSO,

Several Remarkable Interpositions of Divine Providence, in preserving him from dangers, by sea and land, from 1816 to 1823.

BY JOHN MANN,

AUTHOR OF THE EMIGRANT'S INSTRUCTOR.

GLASGOW,

PRINTED BY ANDREW YOUNG,
150, *Trongate*

1824.

Reprinted by:
Saint Annes Point Press
P.O. Box 691
Fredericton, N.B.
Canada. E3B 4K9

Distributed by:
Arctician Books
P.O. Box 691
Fredericton, N.B.
Canada. E3B 4K9

Canadian Cataloguing in Publication Data

Mann, John.
Travels in North America

Reprint of the 1824 ed. published by A. Young, Glasgow.

ISBN 0-920762-02-6

1. Canada — Description and travel — 1800-1850.*
2. New England — Description and travel — 1775-1865. I. Title.

FC72.M35 1978 917.1'04'3 C79-094071-X
F1013.M35 1978

INTRODUCTION

In the years immediately following the Napoleonic Wars, emigration from the British Isles was on the increase. The war was followed by a depression as wages and prices fell and thousands of labourers and craftsmen were out of work. The efforts of landowners to consolidate their holdings forced many tenants off the land and increased the number of unemployed who crowded the streets of the cities. The situation became more desperate when thousands of veterans were discharged from the army and navy. As a result, in the years 1816-1820, there were many thousands of paupers, unemployed labourers and craftsmen and farmers of "small means" who were eager to take any opportunity of leaving their homeland for America or Australia. At the same time, many people in the British North American colonies felt that their future prosperity depended on a steady influx of healthy immigrants to settle wilderness lands and to provide the labour force for developing industries like the timber trade. This was especially true in New Brunswick where there had been no major influx of population since the arrival of the loyalists in 1783 and the general feeling in the province was that something had to be done to attract settlers.

As a result, the New Brunswick government embarked upon its first major effort to encourage immigration to the province. In May 1816, the House of Assembly decided it was necessary to provide some form of assistance to settlers, and they agreed to provide £1000 for this purpose. In June the government entered into an agreement with James Taylor of Fredericton, who, for the sum of £1000, agreed to bring 134 settlers from Scotland. All were to be under age 40 and 100 were to be adults over 15. Infants under two were not counted and two children between two and ten were to be counted as one adult. All were to have certificates of good character signed by a minister and all were to be in good health. Taylor chartered a new ship, the *Favorite* of Saint John, and early in October 1816 Scottish newspapers reported that the ship was in the Clyde and that people wishing to settle in New Brunswick would be given a passage free of charge. Unmarried men and women were preferred since it was felt that New Brunswick needed strong young labourers and domestic servants.

Taylor's contract required that he land his settlers in Saint John by December 1, 1816, so the vessel was loaded very quickly. Several married men even agreed to pay for a passage for themselves and their families. They were later reembursed by the New Brunswick government who considered them as good settlers as those given a free passage. The passenger list contains 136 names, including a number of children and there were also the usual few stowaways. One infant died on the voyage and one man returned in the vessel to Scotland.

After a relatively short passage of what appears to have been 24 days, the *Favorite* reached the Bay of Fundy and stopped at the quarantine grounds off Partridge Island. On November 22, she docked in Saint John where the passengers, most of whom were destitute, were landed. One of these passengers was John Mann, the author of this book.

John Mann was not the type of person usually thought of when describing authors of 19th century travel narratives. He was not a well educated gentleman or a professional soldier travelling for excitement or to broaden his knowledge of the world, nor was he a cleric out to bring light to the backwoods settlements of British North America, or full of missionary zeal to civilize the "heathen" Indians. According to the passenger list of the *Favorite,* Mann was an eighteen year old labourer from Kenmore at the head of Lock Tay in Perthshire Scotland, and the book he produced is the simple narrative of a literate but plain man, possessed of intelligence, a sense of adventure, a restless spirit and an ability to describe events and scenes which he hoped would appeal to his readers. The bulk of his narrative deals with his experiences in New Brunswick and in travelling to and from the province. It is one of the earliest works dealing with New Brunswick and it contains interesting information about immigration, the force which more than any other was to determine the future development of the province and its character down to the present time. Mann's narrative merits reprinting since it is extremely rare and it is found in very few libraries or private collections. It was published in Glasgow in 1824 at the same time as a second work by Mann, entitled *The*

Imigrant's Instructor, which is a guide for settlers intending to immigrate to New Brunswick, Canada or New York.

The Emigrant's Instructor is perhaps not as interesting as Mann's *Travels,* but it does contain useful information and it is a pity that Mann did not combine the two into one substantial book. Both books certainly lack polish and Mann's grammar is far from faultless. The *Travels* contains a number of factual and spelling errors. The most obvious error is the spelling of Massachusetts on the title page, but this error is not as great as is the spelling of Partridge Island as found on page eight. However, the errors are minor and the book is reprinted here exactly as it appeared in 1824.

The early section of Mann's book deals with the voyage of the *Favorite* from Greenock and its arrival at Saint John. This is the earliest account located of the actual passage of an immigrant ship to New Brunswick. It contains a short but useful description of conditions on board such vessels in a period in which the Passengers' Act, which was supposedly designed to protect passengers, was in fact very ineffective since there was little attempt made to enforce it. However, conditions on board the *Favorite* were actually better than on many vessels in this period. Probably, this was because Taylor was being paid well to bring out only 134 settlers, which meant there was no need for the overcrowding that was common on many vessels. The captain also enforced some sanitary regulations and made the passengers vacate their berths regularly so they could be cleaned, something which was often ignored by many masters. For these reasons there was very little sickness on the *Favorite,* except the usual seasickness, and only one death, that of an infant. However, Mann does describe a practice followed by the master, which was common on emigrant ships, and that was to feed the passengers well on the first day with lots of porridge and molasses which made them sick early in the voyage. This meant they would use fewer provisions later and, since the master or shipowner was required to furnish certain quantities of food and water, money could be saved this way. However, Mann gives no indication that there was ever a shortage of provisions or water, which was often the case on vessels, and occasionally immigrants landed virtually in a state of starvation.

Another common practice of Brokers, Ships' Agents, and Masters was to mislead immigrants by offering them passages to places which were far from their destinations, telling them for example that they should take a cheap passage to Miramichi, Saint John or St. Andrews, since these ports were within easy travelling distance of Boston, Quebec, New York and Philadelphia. Occasionally they would show the immigrant these places on a map, the scale of the map being so small that New York would appear to be right next door to St. John. Usually the poor immigrant had no idea where these places were only that he had a relative or friend there. In many cases the master was not at all concerned about the fate of passengers trying to reach Quebec whom he dropped off somewhere in New Brunswick. Many masters and shipowners were only in the immigrant trade to make a quick profit and they used many types of deception to attract passengers and they often cheated them in any way they could. This was especially true in the early decades of the 19th century. It is also true that there were many humane and generous masters who did all they could to help their passengers.

Mann and the passengers on the *Favorite* did not face any of the problems just described, but he does describe his encounters with people who did, such as the two Irishmen whom he met walking from Quebec to New Brunswick, accompanied by their wives and two tiny children, with no idea of the distance they had to travel or of the difficulties they would have to face. In this period the colonial governments occasionally gave small grants to settlers located in remote places on main routes of travel like Lake Temiscouta and Grand Falls on the upper reaches of the St. John river. These grants were to provide some form of shelter and food for travellers, many of whom could not afford to pay for such help. One such settler was John Long at Lake Temiscouta and another was Charles Stewart at Grand Falls, who between August 1822 and March 1823, aided over sixty people. Mann describes his visits to the homes of some of these hardy pioneers, including a visit to the home of John Long, although he does not mention Long by name.

Mann was not very impressed with New Brunswick and on his arrival in Charlotte County in the winter of 1816, he was shocked at what he considered "the dismal and wretched appearance" of the country. He considered it a "most excellent place of banishment". Unfortunately he does not say how he survived the winter of 1816. However, passengers landed as late in the season as those who came in the *Favorite,* usually had difficulty finding work and many ended up in the Alms House in Saint John or were looked after in private lodgings paid for by the Overseers of the Poor. In later years, when immigration to New Brunswick was regulated a little more closely, it was usual to charge masters or shipowners a head tax on every immigrant landed. This money was used to defray the expense of looking after those who needed aid. After 1848 the head tax was doubled for those landed after September 1st because it was found that those landed so late in the year usually needed assistance all winter. This was certainly the case for many of those landed from the *Favorite* and in 1816 there was no head tax to provide funds for their welfare. Aid was certainly necessary and whether or not the government assisted all these settlers is unclear, but they did provide funds to aid married men with families. It was thought that able-bodied single men could look after themselves. Mann may have been one of those aided although there are no records to prove this. The next summer, he followed the usual custom for immigrants who did not have the capital to locate on lands of their own; he went to work loading lumber boats and cutting timber. Unhappy with his situation, but unable to leave because of a lack of money, he was forced to spend a second winter on the Magaguadavic. He does not say much about this period except to describe several drownings he witnessed as well as his own narrow escapes from death.

Mann visited Saint John in the summer of 1819 and this gave him an opportunity of witnessing another type of immigration. In the years 1816-1820, many British regiments were being disbanded and the British government was eager to have many of these men settle in the colonies. As a result, a number of regiments such as the 104th, the 98th and the New Brunswick Fencibles, were disbanded in New Brunswick and given land grants in various parts of the province. One such regiments was the West Indies Rangers, a tough unit which included deserters and outcasts from other regiments. In April

1819, the Executive Council was informed that the Rangers were to be disbanded in New Brunswick. Mann describes vividly the excitment in Saint John when the soldiers were landed in June, (not January as Mann says) 1819. They were given their severance pay and let loose in the streets. Mann describes those scenes which he thought would interest his readers. Perhaps his account is a bit over-blown but it can be verified to a certain extent by newspaper accounts, and the Common Council of Saint John did in fact petition the government to prevent the landing of these troops. They feared the consequences of turning them loose in a city which in a ten day period had seen the arrival of over 2000 immigrants, most of whom were destitute and wandering the streets. The city officials certainly expected trouble and Mann describes what he saw. What he does not mention is that the regiment contained many respectable officers and men, many of whom were to settle down very shortly on lands on the upper reaches of the St. John river near the men disbanded earlier from some of the other regiments. These ex-soldiers became very useful in opening this area for settlement and they were encouraged by the government who felt they were ideal people to settle near the border with the United States in case of the outbreak of another war. Mann mentions that he met some of these men in his travels on the river.

Mann left Saint John to spend the rest of the summer of 1819 as a member of the surveying party under William F. Odell, who was working with the commission attempting to determine the boundary between Maine and New Brunswick. Odell was not the Surveyor General as Mann says; he was the Provincial Secretary from 1818 to 1844, but in 1819 he had been released from his duties so he could take charge of the survey. Mann does not give many details of the work carried out, except for a brief description of the survey done on Mars Hill opposite Woodstock. He does give some information on the size of the party and, as usual, he gives detailed descriptions of the journey up and down the river, with more narrow escapes from death. He also describes, briefly, a visit to the Indian village at Kingsclear with an amusing description of the beaver and its habits. The commission was unable to settle the boundary question at this time and in September the party was back at Fredericton and Mann was unemployed once more. He travelled overland from Oromocto to the Magaguadavic where he remained with relatives until the summer of 1822. Mann gives no information about this period, but he does imply that he found life in Charlotte county rather boring. By 1822, he was dissatisfied with New Brunswick and having heard of the "fame of Canada", he decided to pay that place a visit. This was not unusual for immigrants and in the first half of the 19th century roughly 50% of all those who landed in New Brunswick from the British Isles moved to the United States or Canada, many staying only long enough to find a passage to Boston or Quebec, and others like the Irish immigrants Mann met, who had no money, set out to walk to their destinations. Others, like Mann, stayed for a year or two or even longer and then when they had accumulated enough capital or when they had become discouraged over their inability to obtain land of their own, they moved on looking for greener pastures. Conditions were not that much better elsewhere, especially in the United States, and the British consul in New York in the years 1817 to 1819 forwarded a number of unhappy immigrants to Upper Canada, many of whom had come to New York from New Brunswick and Nova Scotia.

Mann spends considerable time describing his travels in 1822 which began in June at Eastport. From Eastport he travelled to Portland and he gives a detailed description of a fire he witnessed there which destroyed 20 buildings. His description of his journey through New York to Upper Canada is little more than a list of places visited with the distances between them, but his stay in Upper Canada provided him with opportunities to record a few stories, all of which clearly indicate the poverty of most settlers and the isolation of the settlements he visited. Conditions seem to have been much like those in New Brunswick and Mann was not favourably impressed. He pushed on to Montreal and Quebec before returning to New Brunswick in September 1822. Unfortunately he provides few details concerning his travels from Upper Canada to Quebec, and his description of his journey along the banks of the St. Lawrence contains mainly accounts of his problems in making himself understood so as to obtain food and lodgings. He enlivens his account with a description of a funeral in Montreal and of a party in a French Canadian village. His description of his passage from the St. Lawrence to the St. John river is much more detailed and contains remarks about the travellers he met, the places where he obtained food and a bed, and the Indians with whom he travelled for a while.

When Mann returned to New Brunswick, he still could not settle down. He spent another winter in Charlotte county and then decided to pay a visit to Scotland. It is not clear whether or not he intended to stay, but his book ends with a statement that he had expected to find happiness in Scotland but that if it ever was there it was gone.

Further details of Mann's life are very sketchy. For some reason he must have decided that his best hope was back in Charlotte county, that "most excellent place for banishment", and he settled down in the Parish of St. George. When he returned is not certain, but his oldest daughter was born in New Brunswick in 1829. In the 1851 census, Mann was residing in the same parish with a wife and seven children. His books apparently were not circulated very widely and there are no records of his ever attempting to publish anything more. He lived to the ripe old age of 92 and died 19 February, 1891.

John Mann's *Travels* is an excellent source for information on travel conditions in New Brunswick in a period when much of the province was uninhabited or very sparsely inhabited. Mann may seem to exaggerate the hardships he encountered. However, letters and reports can be found such as those of surveyor Dugald Campbell which provide descriptions which differ very little from those of Mann, although they are not nearly as colourful or as entertaining. Mann's *Travels* certainly belong in the collection of anyone interested in the early history of New Brunswick. It is a unique and valuable book.

W. A. Spray
St. Thomas University
Fredericton, N.B.

PREFACE

The Author of the following narrative, who is a native of the parish of Kenmore in Perthshire, emigrated to America in the year 1816, with the intention of settling the Province of New-Brunswick. After a residence of a few years in that quarter, he became dissatisfied with the privileges he enjoyed there, and proposed to some of his associates, (who were also discontented with their situation,) to take a tour through part of the United States, to Upper Canada, in order to ascertain the situation and local circumstances of the inhabitants of the different New Settlements in that Province. But as his associates, being few in number, were unwilling to expend any sum in such an uncertain undertaking; he undertook the journey himself, and wrote a simple statement of all that befel him, and of the most particular objects that were presented to his view; in hopes of defraying his expenses in another way.

After travelling a circuit of *One thousand Nine hundred and Seventy Miles,* and having previously accompanied the Surveyor-General of New-Brunswick, when exploring extensive and solitary deserts, at the time of drawing the line between the British and American territories, he deemed it prudent, after his arrival in Scotland, to publish a pamphlet, entitled "The Emigrant's Instructor;" but as that pamphlet was published chiefly for the benefit of intending Emigrants, he thought it unnecessary to insert all the particulars of his adventures; which, at the request of several respectable individuals, he is induced now to present to the public; and he trusts they will be read with general satisfaction, and will prove interesting, and even profitable, to those who, from the prospect of acquiring riches, have a desire to leave their native country.

TRAVELS, &c.

Voyage from Port-Glasgow in Scotland, to St. John's in New Brunswick.

I SAILED from Port-Glasgow, on the 22d day of October, 1816, in the Ship Favourite, of St. John's, bound for that place, with upwards of a hundred passengers, chiefly from Perthshire. The ship was hired by the Governor of New Brunswick, for the purpose of carrying Scotch Settlers into that quarter: who had to procure proper certificates of their character, signed by the ministers of their respective parishes, and also by a Justice of Peace. We remained three days at the banks, during which time several persons came on board, concealing themselves amongst the passengers, expecting to get their passage without being discovered. The Captain and Owner having been ashore, when they came on board, the passengers were ordered upon deck, a rope was fixed across the quarter deck, and all the passengers were called one by one to stand behind the rope. The vessel being then searched, some of the characters just mentioned, were found amongst the chests, and some in the forecastle, and one was even found rolled in the fore-topsail. Being discovered, they were all sent ashore, but some of them returned that same night. Though the vessel was searched several times, yet after we sailed, there were found several individuals of this description, who had always stolen on board during night; and being chiefly seamen, the vessel was consequently well manned.

On the 25th, during a pleasant and favourable gale, we weighed anchor. We were allowed porridge and molasses for breakfast. The Captain, well knowing the effects of the latter, supplied us the first day with double the quantity of our allowance. We being ignorant of its tendency and operation, drank heartily of it. One of the passengers who had been at sea before, said, "You will curse the molasses yet." Towards the middle of the day the wind began to blow hard, the vessel to be tossed, and the molasses, heavy upon the stomach, began to operate; so that the most part had to crawl upon deck, in order to discharge the quantity drunk, overboard; others that were too lazy in ascending upon deck had to get buckets where they lay. This breeze continued three days, during which time we took little or nothing of the provision belonging to the ship; and as for the molasses, we tasted no more of it during the passage. We were divided into messes, each mess containing eight persons; and our allowances of beef, bread, and oatmeal, were weighed to us every day. To prevent disputing and quarreling, a small piece of wood was fixed to each piece of beef, with the number of the mess marked upon it, and all put in the same plate. Very few however could take regular diets, or make use of their allowance, when it blew hard; so that they lived more upon the supplies they had of their own, than on the ship's provisions, until they properly recovered from the sea sickness. When fully restored, once in two days, we were all ordered upon deck, bedding and all, and the births were sprinkled over with vinegar.

When our voyage was about half finished, the sailors, in order to procure some whisky from the passengers, asked liberty of the Captain to shave the passengers, as if they were crossing the line. This practice is prevalent among sailors going to the West Indies. Any person that never crossed the line before must be shaven by Neptune. He comes on board and inquires, "Are there any of my children here?" Those who were shaven before and who wish to see the ceremony repeated, tell him that there are; and then they secure the individual that is to be shaven, and bind him on deck: one of themselves acting Neptune, mixes some tar and other ingredients together for lather, and besmears the face of the person who is to endure the operation with this composition. Questions are proposed to him, to which he must give distinct replies, and instantly when he opens his mouth, Neptune puts some of this mixture into it. Then he takes for a razor an iron hoop, and commences the operation of shaving; and the more the individual objects to the ceremony, the more cruelty he experiences from his rigid Father: but on promising so much liquor, he is treated with less severity. Towards the end of the ceremony, he is requested never to row when he can sail, &c. When extricated, he washes himself in the long boat, which is filled with salt water for that purpose. They had a practice of washing them long ago, by throwing them overboard, and hauling them by means of a rope under the vessel, from the one side to the other. It is reported, that some had been drowned in this way, and then a stop was put to that abominable practice. The Captain gave the sailors liberty to shave the passengers; but they, knowing that it was never a custom in going to North America, stoutly resisted it. We all stood upon the quarter deck, while the sailors were making ready. They got the long boat half filled with water, stripped off their clothes, (except their shirts and trowsers,) each having a short club; and Neptune with a false face, and a four pronged fork in his hand. They all advanced toward us determined to overcome us by force, being all stout and inured veterans. We were more than double their number, but not near so regular in strength, nor so uniform. One of the passengers cried out, "Let us not forfeit to-day the renown which the ancient High-Landers gained of old." Another pointing his dirk at the sailors said, "If you proceed any farther, I shall have some of your lives." The Captain on seeing this commotion was terrified, and though he had given them liberty a little ago, aware of the consequences, he solicited them to drop the intended operation, but finding them resolute at first, he says, "I wish I had you all ashore," but after entreating them a second time, they were reconciled, and abandoned their abominable project.

After nineteen days' sailing, we observed land not far from us, being some desolate Island. The wind was fair this whole period, but the next morning it blew a tremendous gale, which continued forty-eight hours. The first day we bore S. W., but at last we were under the necessity of heaving her up in the wind, under close riefed top-sails, and a middle stay-sail, until the wind abated. Then we sailed northward for the land again, and in the course of two days we reached the Bay of Funday. A thick fog came on then, which compelled us to remain there during two days, for fear of being cast on some rocks, or Island. After the fog was dispelled, we got sight of Grandmannon: the wind being S. W., we had a good run-up to the anchorage at Patriga Island, which is within two miles of the city. The Captain, Owner, and four hands went ashore in the boat, and returned about ten o'clock that same evening. The sailors who went ashore drank rather free in the city, and brought some spirits on board to their comrades; then all had wet the other eye, and began to quarrel. The Captain attempted to quell their disputes, but instead of succeeding, they were more obstreperous and refractory in consequence of his interference. They unanimously beated and abused him, and the rest of the officers: he threatened them with fire-arms, but they snatched the pistol he had in his hand, knocked him down upon deck, and had in contemplation to shoot him. He with difficulty made his way into his cabin and bolted the door. They were just on the eve of breaking it open with the intention of killing him, when instantly some person on deck with a most pitiable tone, exclaimed, "All hands upon deck to save the cabin!" At these words, all the passengers immediately put on their clothes, as expeditiously as they could: breaking a long ladder in splinters, each taking a piece in his hand, they appeared instantly on deck. The sailors at this time went down to the fore-castle, as it was conjectured, to prepare for action. We were informed that they had two muskets and some pistols; that they intended to murder the Captain, to cut the cable, and to run off with the ship. To prevent this dreadful attempt, we all stood upon the quarter deck, some with staves, and some with edged tools, splinters of the ladder, or whatever instruments we could get hold of. A schooner passed us at no great distance, to which we made a signal for relief, but owing to the storm and the darkness of the night, those on board did not hear us. Then the mate and four hands made off to the light-house to make known our distressing circumstances. A signal was immediately fired, which was instantly answered from the Fort, and in less than half an hour, two boats, full of officers and soldiers, were alongside. The sailors by this time had fallen asleep, through excess of drink. The chief officer ordered the ringleaders of the mutiny to be brought forward. Four of them were then put in irons, and were committed to two constables till the day appointed for their trial. The Captain was fined, and the sailors liberated. One of them afterwards met him on the street, knocked him down, and then disappeared.

The bounds of this Narrative will not permit me to mention the various accidents which happened during this voyage, though I carefully noted every particular in my journal.

Remaining a few days in the city of St. John, I went on board a small vessel which was bound for St. Andrew's. We were only three days on the voyage, two of which we anchored at Eastport. Proceeding from thence, I came to the river Magegadavick, where I remained for some time.

On land here, I was shocked at the dismal and wretched appearance of the country. From the severity of the winter, and the gloomy aspect which the woods and water presented, one would certainly conclude this to be a most excellent place for banishment. I spent a part of the winter at the river Magegadavick, and the remainder near Scrodiac.

Once, as I was sailing from the one river to the other, my companions and I went ashore upon the American side, to visit some Indian wigwams. We were not a little surprised on seeing their manner of nursing their papose;* nor were we less surprised on seeing one of the women who was in the boat with us, resting herself in one of the wigwams, and eating some shell-fish, raw or alive, just as it was taken out of the mud.

About the first settlement of this country, an old lady who lived near St. Andrew's, dreamed of her neighbouring landlady having her child boiling in the pot. Next morning the old lady went to visit them, and knowing that she had no provisions, and observing a pot boiling on the fire, inquired what it contained. At first they were unwilling to reply, but being solicited, they at length acknowledged that they were driven by necessity to cook a dead dog, which was suspended before the door for some days before.

---

*See the Emigrant's Instructor, Page 44.

I was chiefly employed during the following summer, in loading vessels with tun-timber for Britain. Being one day in the woods cutting spars with a ship carpenter, I cut down one, and was lopping off one of the branches, when a hidden slim tree, which the limbs of the spar brought to the ground, sprung up, struck me on the face, and drove me backwards my whole length, where I lay weltering in blood, until the carpenter, who was at a distance, came to my assistance, and carried me to the boat, in which I was sent on board the ship, until I recovered.

One night as I was going to bed from the forecastle along the beams, I suddenly fell down head foremost into the hold. Fortunately my head escaped being hurt by a square block of timber, which lay in the bottom of the ship; my shoulders struck upon the edge of it. Those in the cabin and fore-castle perceived the vessel shaking, but were ignorant of the cause until some of them came to ascertain it. I felt the effects of this fall, for about a week or ten days.

In the fall of the year, being displeased with my situation, I was determined to leave the country and go to Canada, but was prevented both from want of means and courage. I was under the necessity of continuing during another winter in the same quarter.

January 1818, during my residence near the river Magegadavick, an accident occurred which I cannot forbear to relate. My Landlord was alarmed by a shriek from a vessel at anchor in the river, and upon our running out, we heard one crying that there was a man drowning in the ice. We made all possible speed to the beach, which was about three hundred yards from us. There we observed a man in the ice supported by an oar, exclaiming, "For God's sake make haste." In the midst of our confusion, we were at a loss how we could afford any assistance to him. Seeing a raft of boards near us, we began to drag them along laying them on the surface of the ice for a gangway; and well might I approve of the old saying, "the more hurry the less speed." I was unwilling to wait till we got a sufficient quantity of boards collected, but attempted to rescue the unfortunate individual by stepping on a few of them scarcely supported by the ice. I had the end of a line in my hand, those on the beach pulling the other; standing on the end of the outermost board, that I might fix the line to his arm, while he smiled in the prospect of relief; but the board on which I stood, broke through and sunk, and I almost lost my own life, while endeavouring to preserve that of another. Like the old lady with her only son, my attention was now wholly occupied with my own perilous situation. When those on shore observed me going down, they immediately began to pull the line which was tied round my hand. The ice not being strong, was cut by the line, and I was almost hauled under it, before I could call on them to relieve me. The line being relaxed, and getting on the board again, I was drawn ashore with great danger and difficulty. Several attempts, but all in vain, were made to extricate the other man. He was borne by an oar and the ice for some time, after I got ashore; at last the ice yielding, he disappeared, but it is probable that he was dead before he sunk. His body was found within a few yards of low water mark.

Sailing in a boat to St. Andrew's, I observed three men weighing a small anchor close to a vessel. The anchor stuck fast in the mud, and the warp fastened to the boat; the tide running rapidly, and before they could loose the warp, the boat took the water, and immediately sunk; two of the men were saved by swimming, the third with the boat was lost.

Coming from a general training, in a boat, we met two men advanced in life quite intoxicated, paddling up the river in a small craft resembling the shape of a cradle. After passing them, we heard an alarming cry from the shore; on looking behind us, we saw the craft overturned bottom upwards, and two hats floating down the river.

Two men with their wives were crossing the river on a visit: they hauled their wives on a small sled constructed for that purpose. As they were going along, they observed a spot not sufficiently strong, which they determined to avoid on their return. As they were returning, therefore, and concluding they were not far from the place, they stopt, but just as they were speaking, the ice gave way, and the two wives perished.

A company of youngsters leaving a dancing frolic, were crossing the ice: One of the ladies, apparently dissatisfied that the company dismissed so early, began to dance: the ice yielded, and the unfortunate lady disappeared, bidding adieu to every worldly pleasure.

Considering it unnecessary to swell my narrative with such accidents, I shall proceed to give a relation of my own perils and misfortunes.

In October, 1818, I agreed with Captain Leisk, of the Brig Lion of Aberdeen, for my passage to Grangemouth. Going on board, and sailing over to St. Andrew's, we were obliged to anchor there for five days, on account of a contrary wind. While we stopt here, two of my relations came on board, pressing me to drop my intention of sailing to Scotland, but they could not prevail, as I was determined, if possible, to see my friends that winter. On the 4th of October, we weighed anchor; the wind about W.; sailed out through Lieutect Passage with a fair breeze; but in the afternoon the wind came straight a-head again. So we were obliged to return to Lieutang Harbour that night. The Captain was raging, and swore that the vessel must sail next morning, let the wind be what it will. Accordingly, next morning we weighed anchor, and attempted to beat out, but all to no purpose. I then began to think seriously that there must be something extraordinary in the case, and being considerably agitated in mind, began to contrive how to make an excuse to get ashore. I determined however, if the wind was favourable next morning, to make a third attempt, and if not, to contrive some pretext in order to return. I slept little during that night, contriving what excuse to make to get ashore if the wind was not favourable in the morning; and getting up through the night; I requested two of the boys that kept on anchor watch, to put me ashore on the opposite Island, but they, apprehensive of the consequence, absolutely refused me that favour. I went to bed again, commending myself to the will of Providence; and about day-light looking up, I saw that the wind continued to blow from the same quarter considerably higher than the preceding day, I was then resolved to return. When the Captain came on deck, the Pilot addressing me, said, "This is all your fault, Sir, that we can never get a fair wind," to whom I replied, it must be either yours or mine, so I am willing to cast lots to decide which of us shall go ashore, but he not being disposed to try that experiment, I said I would go ashore without lots. The Captain smiling, said, "my friend, have you given up the ghost?" I replied in the affirmative, and on giving him the letters entrusted to me, I departed, bidding them all farewell.

October the 17th, I went ashore, in the desert near Lieutang River, and steering W., a straight course through the woods. When I came in sight of Megegadavick River, there was a fine gale from the N. W. which was quite favourable for the Brig to leave the land. Then I sat down reflecting whether I had done right or wrong. Some times I thought I had done well to return, as the vessel was very old, crazy and leaky. But considering, on the one hand, that I had now to spend another winter in this detestable cold country, besides what banters I had to suffer for returning: On the other hand, that if I had gone in the Brig, I would see all my friends once more. I was so much harassed and vexed, that I thought it would be better for me to die than to live. I immediately fixed a resolution of leaving that quarter without making my appearance, but not being prepared for the journey, I had no other alternative than to make my appearance. The next day, I crossed the Bay to St. Andrew's, along with some of the inhabitants, and stopt there two days, detained by a violent storm. All the vessels in the harbour struck against each other, and a great quantity of the timber floated down the Bay. The storm was so excessively high, I did not repent my return, being fully persuaded that such a crazy vessel as the Brig was could not withstand it. Seeing the Pilot in St. Andrew's, he informed me that on the very day I left the vessel, she got by West Quady, then he withdrew and got ashore. The Brig was never heard of, and in all probability, was lost with all on board.

January 1819, travelling from the River St. Croix to Degidequash and Magegadavick, in company with a friend; but night overtaking us, and observing a house that had a very good appearance close by the road side, we called for lodgings. The landlady refused to accommodate us, alleging those employed in the woods were expected, and she could not entertain us. We were informed that there was a house a little distance before us, in which we might procure lodgings. We were very reluctant to remove, being fatigued with travelling among deep snow. There was no alternative: we marched to the house alluded to, found the occupants (newly arrived from Ireland) in the most wretched circumstances: Some of the family confined by indisposition, and some by the fire-side, without any appearance either of food or clothing. Getting no accommodation here, we had to return and encounter a second time with the old lady, who, if she had known our conditions, might easily now overcome us. As she could augur nothing unfavourable from our appearance, and suspecting that we would not be prevailed on to go away a second time, she courteously entertained us, and accommodated us both with lodgings and victuals.

In April, travelling the same way, being on a visit, and expecting to arrive at a certain settlement before night; I carried no refreshment. Towards evening, I was very much exhausted and fatigued in consequence of the deep snow, and began to faint with hunger. I sat down repeatedly, thinking to recruit my strength, and had the greatest difficulty from my faint condition to rise again. My distance from the nearest settlement, precluded the hope of reaching it without refreshment. When I almost despaired of any relief, by Divine Providence I was led to a handful of Indian corn scattered in the mire, which I picked up with the greatest care, and which formed one of the most palatable repasts I have ever taken. In a little, I recovered strength, and was enabled to walk without being under the necessity of resting myself incessantly as formerly. At length, I came to a camp occupied by two men, who shewed me the greatest kindness.

January 11th, 1819, I sailed with the exploring party, from St. Andrew's for St. John's. On landing here, we were not a little surprised to see the whole city in an uproar, occasioned by a party of the West India Rangers, who, being disbanded here, were offered either so much land, or ten pounds in cash. A great part of them preferred the latter. Some of them were preparing for home, and others for the United States. They threw off their regimentals, and were furnishing themselves with coloured clothes. They were not two hours ashore, when the most part of them were quite intoxicated. In this condition, they were disposed to quarrel and contend with every one that met them. Being present where one of them was purchasing a jacket and hat, he presented his purse to the merchant, ordering him to pay himself. When the overplus was returned to the owner, he said, "What shall I do with the bloody dollars, come give me a silk handkerchief, or something for them." Another who had a bundle of clothes by him, requested one of the spectators to help him on with his burden, and rewarded him with a dollar for his trouble. I thought their circumstances justified the intelligence, I often heard in my native country, respecting the liberal wages given to servants, at least in some parts of America. Towards evening, we could scarcely walk the streets with the crowds. One of them stood in the market place, almost naked, challenging to fight any person that came in his way. He threw away his vest on the street, which contained his money, and would have lost the whole contentedly, had not one of his companions who was a little more sober, picked up the dollars which poured from the vest. While he was performing this kind office, the drunken wretch beat him most cruelly: however, for the sake of the dollars, he endured a few blows; and when all were collected he withdrew. At night the inhabitants were obliged to secure their doors, sooner than usual, on account of the rioters. This regiment consisted wholly of deserters, and criminals of various characters, who were sent into it, instead of banishment.

June 17th, we left St. John's; and after two days' rowing and sailing up the river, we arrived at Fredericton, where we met with the Surveyor-General, and the rest of the company. Here we got our skiffs, canoes, provisions, &c., all in readiness; and set off for the river Dishoot, where we expected to meet the American party.

The first day, we made little speed, not being much acquainted with the canoes, and some were overturned. The next day we started very early, passed by an Indian village, but our time would not permit us to visit it, the officers being some distance before us. We strove to overtake them, but without success. The night approaching, we halted at a beach, kindled a fire, and lay down by it all night, having only a single blanket each, with a hard stone for a pillow. Next day, at 10 o'clock, we overtook the officers. We had much difficulty in ascending the Meductic Falls, being very rapid and narrow, and full of large stones, against which the water dashed with such violence, that it seemed truly terrific to approach them. After great and dangerous labour, we all got safe through, and then proceeded, constantly polling, during the space of six days. By this time, we entered into a new Settlement, as we observed, by the stumps and bushes in the fields. We had some difficulty to get a place where to erect our tents, the land being lately granted to soldiers, and only a few trees cut here and there on spots where they intended to build. While we were pitching our tents here, the midges were so vicious that we had to cover our faces with our handkerchiefs to protect us. They would get in under our clothes, and into our very ears. It is impossible to describe what we suffered from these insects, till we got our tents erected, and fire kindled, which was the only expedient for driving them away. When we occasionally went any distance from our tents, we carried a small branch of cedar bark in our hands, having the one end continually smoking, and keeping it near our face, choosing rather to suffer from the smoke, than from these tormenting insects.

Having now arrived at the river Dishoot, where we expected to meet the American party, we built a small house, to contain our provisions; and expecting to be out late in the fall, we returned again to Fredericton, for another cargo. The distance was 100 miles. By paddling some times, and at other times lying down in the bottom of the canoes, while floating down the rapid current, in less than three days we arrived at Fredericton.

After getting our cargo, we proceeded to the appointed place, with more experience in the practice of polling. Passing the Indian village before-mentioned, we went ashore to visit the inhabitants. As we proceeded to their wigwams, we met a young Indian, with his bow and arrow. He employed himself in aiming at a halfpenny; expecting, no doubt, that we would set up more for him. Every copper we set up, he succeeded to hit with his arrow, though at some distance, and then put it into his pocket. By his dexterity, he deprived us of all the coppers we carried. On entering one of the wigwams, the landlord told us he had a young beaver, which we were very anxious to see. He promised us a sight of it for some money; after paying which, he introduced it.*

After visiting the wigwams, we took a view of the Church. The Priest, (a Frenchman,) who lived in a small house at the end of the Chapel, without a living creature beside him, came out. We asked him if we might be allowed to see the inside of the Chapel. He shook his head, signifying that he had no English: but by means of signs, we made him sensible of our intention, and then he immediately opened the door. The inside was neatly finished with plain work. The pulpit was erected in one end, and a number of images and printed papers were pasted on the front of it, but we could make nothing of their contents. After gratifying our curiosity in this village, we departed; and after a day's hard toiling, we encamped on the banks of the river. Here I was seized with the cramp, which rendered me unfit for service. Next morning I agreed with one Mr. Smith, to convey me to his house, thirty miles up the river. When I entered the boat, my complaint was considerably alleviated, and towards evening, I felt myself recovering fast, yet I remained in the boat till we arrived at his house. When his family retired to rest, I expected my friend would direct me to a bed,

---

*This animal is about the size of a small dog, of a dark colour, and has a small head, and sharp nose and teeth: Its tail resembles, in shape, a man's hand, and is as hard as leather. In running streams, these creatures will make large dams, by means of small trees, which they cut with their teeth, and lay them across the brook, filling the vacancies with small sticks and clay, the tail serving for a shovel, or trowel. Among this they build beds to themselves, so as to answer their purpose whether the water be high or low: Here they bring forth their young. They live upon trouts, which they catch in these dams. In the winter season, they cut holes in the ice, through which they get above the water, and wander abroad, leaving one at the hole, stirring it with its tail, to keep it from freezing, in case of being alarmed, till they all return, after their excursion.

but he withdrew, apparently unconcerned about me. Soon after, the landlady appeared with an old blanket, in which I was to lie on the floor. Such accommodation did not really suit my present condition. I said nothing, and she retired. At length, a servant boy, who was just going up stairs to bed, said, "Please come away with me, Sir. What manner of using strangers is that!" I cheerfully accepted the offer, and slept very comfortably all night. Next day, being thoroughly recovered, I joined the party again, as they passed that way, and after three days we arrived at our intended place of encampment.

One night at bed-time, while we lodged in the hut built for our provision, Mr. Smith, and the boy who offered me a share of his bed, came to our tent, asking lodgings, the night being too far advanced for them to proceed any farther. I requested the boy to sleep with me, reminding him that I was under obligations to show him kindness; but I allowed his master to shift for himself, thinking it might be a lesson to him how to use strangers in future. Some of the company requested him to sleep with the cook, who was a negro, with whom Mr. Smith was under the necessity of passing the night.

During the time we were bringing the second load of provisions, the American party arrived, having come from the State of Vermont, down the St. Lawrence, and the St. John. They encamped at the river Roosthook, fifteen miles above the Dishoot, for which we immediately embarked.

By the time we arrived, they were all prepared to set off with their canoes. The river here run so rapid at the foot of the several cataracts, that we had to carry our canoes and provisions, till we got above the falls. Polling up a violent and rapid current, we allowed the most expert polemen to take the van, and after getting their canoes into still water, they had to return to assist us in getting through. I was among the worst, and had to go on shore, my place being supplied with a more experienced hand; but after all their efforts, one canoe was filled with water, and another was overset, and one of the men's knapsacks and jacket floated down the river. Being more expert at swimming than at polling, I succeeded in bringing the knapsack ashore, but the jacket disappeared before I could reach it.

Ascending the river, (which was but shallow,) I never witnessed such abundance of trouts, some of them of great size. The river being low, they gathered in the deepest holes in crowds, so that we could catch as many as we chose. We fixed three hooks, each pointing in a different direction, laid them down quietly, and when the fish collected in clusters above them, by pulling the hook quick, we caught very many: some fixed in the head, some in the tail, and in other parts of the body. At first we relished them well, but being so fresh they soon became unpalatable. Meeting with a salmon hole, two of our best spearmen went with their canoes, spears, and torches, and killed thirty-seven in the same hole in one night. We put them in a barrel full of pickle taken off the pork, but it was not sufficient to cure them, and being far from any Settlement, we were obliged to throw them into the river.

The American party met us on their return, and informed us, that it was impossible to get to the Penobscot in that direction, as the water was so low. Our General, dissatisfied with this information, ordered us to proceed. We had to leave part of the provisions on the way, as we could not carry them at one load. We cut down a large pine tree, of which we made a canoe to enable us to carry the more with us. As we had one before, called the Royal George, we called the new one the Prince Regent. Before we got it finished, two of the company whom we had left behind, came with another one which they had constructed, but far inferior to the Prince Regent; we then carried all our provision at one load. The number of canoes and men were as follows;—

1 Birch Canoe,	wherein were O.Dell, Surveyor-General, and servant, ...	2
1 Do.	C. Campbell, Commissary, and Do.	2
1 Do.	Cladder, and Do.	2
2 Skiffs,	2 Towmen in each, ...	4
3 Log Canoes,	2 Towmen in each, ...	6
4 Do.	one man each, ...	4
1 Do.	Watson, Commissary, and towmen, ...	3
13 Canoes	Total	23 men

At every encampment, we found plenty of tall grass on the banks of the river, of which I could, in ten minutes, cut with my knife, as much as would serve the whole company for bedding.

About eighty miles from the mouth of the river, we came to a place where it was divided into two branches. We took the left hand branch, on which we proceeded eight miles farther. The river then became so shallow, that we were obliged to haul our canoes half the time upon the bare sand. Being then ninety-four miles from any house or settlement, and unable to proceed any father towards the Penobscot, the officers deemed it prudent to return, and take observations on a small mountain which we passed in coming up the river.

One morning being the 17th of August, as were were preparing for dragging our canoes up the stream we were ordered to turn them down the stream which we immediately obeyed, and cheerfully proceeded down the river. When we got down opposite to the mountain, we encamped on the bank of the river; and next day went to its top, which was covered with wood. We commenced working, and cut down about three acres of the wood; which being done, we erected a scaffold of twenty feet high, from which our officer took the necessary observations. Some of us climbed a high spruce tree, from which we had a view as far as the eye could reach, of a desert, excepting one mountain which was situated westward, and naturally bare.

Descending the mountain, we entered our canoes but the water being low, we had to drag them even with the stream: and after a few days toiling in this manner, we arrived at the place already mentioned called Carrying Place, where we turned our canoes and skiffs bottom upwards, and next morning (the 24th August,) they were all covered over with hoar-frost. When we got our baggage across, the two skiffs, and one canoe, were sent with part of the remaining provision to the grand falls at St. John's river, and the rest proceeded to Fredericton. On approaching the first Settlement, some went ashore for milk, which was a great rarity, being so long without seeing a house, or settlement.

Paddling down the river at full speed, some of the people ashore shouted to us, asking, if any of us were disposed to engage for service, but we were so anxious and eager to get home, and thinking ourselves above the station of servants, we scarcely returned them a civil answer. We continued our career down the river till night overtook us, and then went ashore, collected a quantity of old roots and stumps on the bank of the river, and kindled a fire. After supper some lay by the fire-side, and some under the shelter of a hay-stack, where we slept comfortably all night. As soon as day-light appeared, we entered our canoes, and the wind being fair, every one put up his blanket for a sail, and as there were two in each canoe the one held it stretched, while the other steered with the paddles. Approaching the Meductic Falls, we lowered our sails till we got through, and then hoisted them again, and kept them up till we arrived at Fredericton. The Governor was standing on the beach, when our small fleet under full sail advanced to the town. After taking our baggage ashore, we piled all the canoes in a heap, prepared for the next expedition. Then we were paid off, allowance for provision and wages being given us till we reached home. We converted the provision into money, and prepared for our journey.

Left Fredericton at day-light, and after passing several delightful farms on the western side of the river, we came to the Oromocto, where we left the St. John. The day was extremely rainy, and no house or place of shelter could be found till we travelled about seven miles in the desert, where there was a small Settlement, consisting of four or five houses; here we got refreshment, and rested ourselves till the day cleared, and then marched to the next Settlement, which was nine miles distant from where we lodged that night. The next day we travelled on through the desert, carrying with us a small cag of rum and some biscuit; and in the evening arrived at a Settlement on the Magegadavick river. The next day we travelled to the mouth of the river, distant 80 miles from Fredericton.

By the time we arrived here, (Sept. 20th,) the harvest was finished. The season being excessively dry, the farmers embraced the opportunity of setting fire to all the old stumps in the fields. The wind blew extremely high, so that the different fires communicated together, and the conflagration spread all around, consuming the woods and fences, to the no small danger of several houses in the neighbourhood. The sparks were carried by the wind to the distance of half a mile. One of these struck upon the end of the house in which I lodged, and fell down among some shingles lying at the end of the house. We immediately removed the shingles; but fearing that the house would immediately catch fire, we took out all the furniture, and carried it into the middle of the field, and watched it till about midnight, when the wind and the fire abated.

An unfortunate man, being the worse of liquor, was travelling through the woods, and insensible of his danger, rushed into the fire and smoke. He was found next morning by the road-side, as black as a burnt root, lying on his back, all his clothes being burnt on his body, and his shoes on his feet. His arms, legs, and every part of his body were completely scorched and burnt. As he was so disfigured that he could not be put into a proper coffin, we nailed a few boards together, in that form in which he was lying. We wrapped him in a sheet, and buried him in his own orchard, as is customary in that quarter.

Another fire, at the same time, broke out in Nova Scotia. The wind blowing from the Southward; those on board of a Schooner, sailing along the coast, perceived the fire advancing quicker than they could sail. Several families, cattle, houses, barns, fences, and fields of potatoes, to the distance of 100 miles, were burnt to ashes.

Thankful for getting home safe, I resided amongst my relations until the summer of 1822, during which time I encountered several fatigues and hardships, partly occasioned by the severity of the winter, and the heat of the summer, and partly from the want of roads, having to embark, when I had occasion to go any distance from home.

On one of these occasions, three of us were rowing in a small boat, contiguous to a steep rock, from which a tree, that had been overturned by the wind, was suspended. I was sitting in the stern; and, wishing to avoid the rapid current, kept in close to the rock; and merely for diversion, gave no notice to my companions of the impediment close before them. The bowman's head immediately struck against the limbs of the tree, which caused him and the other man to lean to one side; so that the boat was heeled so much, that she got half full of water, before we could get her rightened: nor could we succeed in taking her ashore till we pushed farther on; when we caught hold of the rock, and pushed the boat ahead, until we came to a shelf, on which we stood and discharged her of the water.

Feeling dissatisfied with my present situation, and hearing the fame of Canada, I formed a resolution of leaving this quarter, and of taking a Tour through the States, towards that country, the following summer.

Accordingly, in the month of June, I went to Eastport, in the State of Maine, in order to procure a passage to Boston or New-York; and finding a sloop bound for Portland and Boston, I agreed with the Captain for a passage thither.

June 11th, 1822—I sailed from Eastport, on board the Liberty, of Portland; the wind blew from the S. W. so that we had great difficulty in getting through the straits of Lieubec. The wind soon after was succeeded by a calm which continued during the whole night.

Next morning the wind was from N. E. by E. and the day very rainy. The billows rose to a great height, and being affected with the sea-sickness, and having no person to attend me, I often wished I had contented myself where I was. Having, however, nobody but myself to blame, I endeavoured to reconcile my mind to my distressing situation, in the best manner I could.

One morning, while sailing under the Province of Maine, the seas being very heavy, and no person happening to be on deck, except the helm's-man, I heard a great noise of a person's feet running upon deck, who instantly cried out, "O my G—d!" at which, though half asleep, I immediately jumped up, not feeling the least sickness; but just as I was ascending the stair, the man put down his head, and said that the main boam bickle was gone: as I had thought it was something of greater consequence, I returned to bed, without lending any assistance. The same person had gone ashore a little afterwards for water, and as he was climbing up the side of the vessel, fell down into the sea. He cried out again in the same manner as before, but no person regarded him, supposing that nothing particular occurred, as he was accustomed, on the most frivolous occasions, to call on the Divine Being to protect him. The Captain accidentally looked over the side, and discovering him, he reached him the end of a rope, before the vessel had left him. We then steered in to Portland, where we remained three days, on account of a violent storm.

On landing here, I went to visit the church-yard, and read several epitaphs and inscriptions on the tombstones, among which were the Memoirs of the Master of His Majesty's Brig Boxer, together with the Master and Lieutenant of a Yankee Frigate, (the Enterprise,) who fought off Portland in 1815: all the three were lying close together. The Boxer was taken, and her dead conveyed into Portland churchyard.

Saturday the 15th—At the north-west corner of the town, some men were blasting rocks near the door of the outermost building. A spark blown by the wind communicated to the house, and before it was observed, the premises were past recovery. The next house was seized, and a general alarm being given, the most of the inhabitants assembled on the spot, in less than ten minutes. By this time, the third building, (a beautiful brick-house,) had caught the fire, to which three water engines were soon applied, and by their means it was preserved. Several buildings, lying behind the former, were gradually seized, to which the engines could not be applied, and by the force of the wind the flying sparks were driven before it; so that, in less than fifteen minutes, there were upwards of twenty buildings all in flames. The fire then communicated itself to the next street, leaving four fine buildings in the corner of the square, by the preserving of the brick-house. Then the engine-men expeditiously advanced between the preserved buildings and the opposite front, and played on the roofs and the side walls, wherever the sparks seemed to threaten the greatest danger. Some were standing on the roofs, with wet blankets to cover the front walls. Others were employed in cutting down the houses contiguous to these on fire. I observed one man standing at the door of his own house, and refusing to permit it to be thrown down; but in less than five minutes the fire broke through the back walls of it, and advanced towards the same buildings which they had previously preserved. All hands then had to retire, leaving the opposite side at the mercy of the devouring element. No language can describe the horrible scene which the town presented at this moment. The streets full of baggage and goods, of every description,—the shrieks of women and children were heard every where,—men were employed in throwing beddings, clothes, and furniture, out at the windows,—beds were torn, feathers were flying through fire and smoke,—waggons, loaded with baggage, were forcing their way through the crowd. The fire continued raging from 10 o'clock, A.M. till sun-set; and there was no prospect of extinguishing it, if the wind did not abate, which happily took place about twillight. Then we formed our ranks, and supplying the engines with water, we succeeded, after tedious labour, to extinguish the flames in one part; the back walls of some brick-houses resisted them in another; so that the whole were soon extinguished.

Next morning I went to view the spot. It presented a dismal appearance: Instead of the fine buildings seen the day before, nothing but burnt brick chimnies, and heaps of ruins, presented themselves to view.

Leaving this place, I sailed for Boston, on the 17th. Nothing particular occurred during the passage, excepting a view of the fishing in Boston Bay. We arrived at Boston on the 18th; and next morning, after taking a view of the city, I set off for Albany, distant 167 miles, which I travelled in five days. The principal towns I met with were Waltham, Worcester, Leicester, Brookfield, North Hampton, and Lebanon Springs. A beautiful cleared country presented itself to view all along the way.

After visiting a few of my countrymen in Albany, I pursued my journey towards Shinactady, and up the Mohawk river, to Amsterdam, (a Dutch Settlement;) thence directed my course to Breadalbane, where I met with a few friends. Making a short stay there, I proceeded to Johnston, where I remained three days with some of my acquaintances. I then set off to Caledonia.

July 1st—I travelled towards Utica, which is situated on both sides of the Grand Canal, distant 96 miles from Albany.

The names of the principal villages lying between Utica and Caledonia, with their distances from one another, are as follow:—

From Utica to New Hartford,	4 miles.
— New Hartford to Westmoreland,	7 miles.
— Westmoreland to Vernon,	6 miles.
— Vernon to Sullivan,	9 miles.
— Sullivan to Manlius,	12 miles.
— Manlius to Onondaga,	10 miles.
— Onondaga to Marelius,	12 miles.
From Marelius to Skiniatles,	6 miles.
— Skiniatles to Aurelius,	12 miles.
— Aurelius to Cayuga,	4 miles.
— Cayuga to Geneva,	14 miles.
— Geneva to Seneca,	7 miles.
— Seneca to Gorham,	5 miles.
— Gorham to Canandagua,	4 miles.
— Canandagua to Bloomfield,	12 miles.
— Bloomfield to Lima,	5 miles.
— Lima to Genesee River,	4 miles.
— Genesee to Caledonia,	5 miles.
Total, from Utica to Caledonia,	138 miles.
From Albany to Utica,	96 miles.
Total, from Albany to Caledonia,	234 miles.

I arrived at Caledonia on the 7th of July, and spent that week amongst my acquaintances, some of whom were not a little surprised at my unexpected visit.

I left Caledonia on July the 15th. By this time the reaping was begun in the Genesee country. I travelled westward through South Hampton and Batavia, to Black Rock at Lake Erie, where I crossed the St. Lawrence, and thence took the stage down to the Falls of Niagara; from whence I proceeded to Burlington Bay, to Esquesing, fifteen miles north of Lake Ontario, where I remained ten days with some of my acquaintances.

From this place, I took a tour through the woods, to view the different new Settlements. After travelling about two miles, I fell in with an old bachelor, being a disbanded soldier, from Ross-shire. He had only a few trees cut down, and boarded himself in a neighbouring house, until he cleared space for a camp.—On advancing a little farther, I came into a small clearing, containing a small log-house, occupied by a young couple, newly married. They had a small field of potatoes, wheat and Indian corn, besides a cow and calf.—About a mile father on, I came into a third clearing, where there was a considerable field of wheat, potatoes, Indian corn, and some onions. I observed the buildings in one corner of the field, to which I advanced; and on my approaching nearer, I observed the landlord standing at the end of the house, taking his breakfast, consisting of porridge and milk: A stump of three feet high served for a table. He made me welcome to take a view of his solitary premises. The house was ten feet in length, and seven in breadth. The bed occupied the back side, from end to end. The fire-place was in the front corner, opposite the foot of the bed. The shelf was opposite to the pillow: It contained little of any kind of earthenware, or even any kind of dishes, excepting a wooden plate, a small tin dish, a horn spoon, and a tinder-box. A small looking-glass, together with a musket, were hung on the side wall. I sat by the fire-side, and could view the fields, from between the logs above the fire. This was the second season that this man had lived in this uncomfortable habitation, without the society of any human being. A cow and a calf formed his only companions, during the most part of that time. I was informed that no less than fifty bachelors, mostly of the same description, were in the same township.—After proceeding a little farther through the woods, I returned to my lodgings, as the evening was now fast approaching. Having to cross two Concessions, and only a foot-path to guide me, I missed it, and could not find it again. The moon shone over the tops of the trees, which was now the only guide I had to direct me. Continuing my course, I thought I would come, through time, to some clearing; but after having travelled until I was really fatigued and discouraged, and making my way through bogs, swamps, and underbrush, I began to contrive how I might sleep secure until day-light. But fearing the bear, and other animals might come and discover me, I continued still pushing on among the trees and shrubs, until at last, to my no small joy, I came into a clearing, from which I found a road that directed me to my lodgings, at which I arrived about mid-night.—Next day, I proceeded in another direction, having a guide; and on my way, I met with a small hut occupied by an old bachelor. The door was shut. The lock consisted of a wooden pin drove into an auger-hole, and fixed to the door with a withe. The barn, adjacent the hut, was constructed of two large pine logs, with holes and shutters. Finding no person about the premises, we departed.

From Esquesing, I marched to little York, distant 40 miles, where I embarked on board the Steam-boat for Kingston, distant 180 miles from York.

On arriving there, I proceeded towards Perth, (72 miles from Kingston,) through the woods, and lodged one night in a house of good appearance, and slept in the skin of a buffalo. After passing through Perth, (a description of which may be seen in the Emigrant's Instructor, page 27,) I retired into the back Settlements, where I met unexpectedly with a number of my old acquaintances. On approaching a house occupied by a family with which I was well acquainted at home, and having a letter to the landlord from his brother, I observed him and one of his neighbours carrying wheat into the barn. The day having the appearance of rain, I went into the house, not wishing to interrupt them. The rest of the family consisted of a young woman with her children, and her mother-in-law. As I entered the house, they suspected that I had escaped in consequence of committing a crime deserving punishment. The old woman asked me whence I came. I told her I was sorry to disoblige her, but that I was not disposed to answer her question. She declared they would not discover to any individual my crime, and that they would try their utmost endeavours to conceal me, if I would inform them what was my trespass. I pretended to be very reluctant to confess it. The old lady said seriously, Perhaps you have hurt some person. I was fully persuaded that she took me for a murderer, although she seemed bashful to ask me directly if that was really the case.

She took at last a very modest way of inquiring it, telling me that she had a son herself who used to quarrel when drinking, and perhaps some accident might have happened me in the like condition. Her son of whom she spoke, was he from whom I had the letter directed to the landlord. I denied that I was a murderer, but as I appeared so dull and heavy, she still retained the same opinion. She went out and informed her son that there was an individual in the house in whose hands she feared some accident had happened. The dinner being ready, he came in, and asked me what countryman I was. I civilly refused to gratify him in that respect. He being no judge of the different dialects, took me for an American, and asked me why I had left my country. I told him I was not disposed to tell every person my reasons. "Then," said he, "it was not for building Churches." I replied, it was not. He requested me to sit near, and take some dinner; at the same time, making me welcome to stay all night. I thanked him, and accepted of his kind proposal, and after dinner, he withdrew to his work. I lay down on a bed; the day being warm, and being fatigued with travelling. The old lady spread a handkerchief over my face, to keep off the flies. After a while, I went out and assisted them in with the wheat and the barley; and when our task was finished, we came in to supper. After supper, the landlord drew nigh to the fire to smoke his pipe. Then I took his brother's letter out of my pocket, and presented it to him. Surprised and astonished, they now all fixed their eyes on me. The landlord immediately laid aside his pipe. All were still and silent, till the letter was read. The stranger, though welcome before, was treated very differently afterwards.

After spending a few days here, I took a tour across Mud Lake, along with an acquaintance. We found a small canoe, in which we crossed. On landing, we met with an old gentleman and his son clearing a piece of land on the border of the Lake. The old gentleman boasted much of the quality of the soil, and went and showed us his boundaries. I really did not envy his good fortune. The land was full of stones, lying in heaps; in some places they were nearly as large as his hut. In other places, we could scarcely walk, in consequence of swamps, bogs, &c. After taking a survey of his possession, we returned to the camp, where we got dinner, and then went to our canoe.

The wind blew somewhat strong, and my comrade would not venture to go. I jumped in the stern, and requested him to sit in the fore-part, till we saw how we could manage her, and if we found it dangerous that we would not proceed. He was still very loath to venture in, although near the shore; but after he entered in, I pushed her off, and told him to rest contented. Not daring to move, he sat down in the bottom, desiring me not to venture out. After much labour, we gained the other side. On landing, my companion went in to an Irishman's hut to smoke. It was then approaching towards night, and having six miles to travel, we marched expeditiously through the woods. When it was just dark, my companion was seized with flatulent pains, and told me he could travel no farther. We entered into a small hut, occupied by an Irishman, and asked for lodgings. They told us they could not possibly accommodate us, as they had neither spare beds nor blankets. We replied, that we would content ourselves to sleep on a small quantity of straw, by the fire-side, or in the barn; but, not disposed to entertain us, they always found some excuse to deny us. I asked a drink of water; my comrade begged for a little milk, which, while he was drinking, I received a bare tea cupful of water. It was so thick and muddy, that I scarcely knew whether I was to drink or to eat it. I found it was not safe to take it, and I threw it out at the door. I then started, and ordered my companion to accompany me, even if we should be compelled to sleep in a bush all night. We then marched along at a slow pace. The night was so dark that it was with the utmost difficulty, we made out the road among the trees: After a tedious journey, about midnight, we arrived at the premises of my companion.

After visiting the back Settlements here, I again passed through Perth, and set off for Glengary, distant 120 miles. I made the journey in three days, during which nothing of any importance occurred to me.

On arriving at a house in the Indian Reserve, the occupants of which I knew perfectly well, the landlady was cutting grass at a small distance from the house, and the landlord was attending the cattle. Being unwell and fatigued, I asked liberty of the landlady to go to the house to rest myself a while, which she immediately granted. I went in and laid myself upon a bed. The children were playing about the fire-side, whose noise deprived me of the repose I wished. The landlady soon came in, to whom I offered a few dollars I carried, and desired her to serve and attend me until I recovered, but she refused to take any charge, until such time as she would consult her husband. She appeared to feel sorry for my condition, but few words passed until the landlord came. She then told him of my situation; but he suspected that I was an imposter. He then began to question me, but he could make nothing of me. He desired his wife to bring a candle, but he could not from my features ascertain who I was. The landlady approaching near, was convinced in her suspicion, and declared she knew my face perfectly well. I could not gratify them by conversation until I recovered.

The next day he accompanied me to visit one of his neighbours, who had newly settled here. The house of this individual was about twelve feet in length, and ten in breadth. It contained only one bed occupying the whole length of the house, in which all the family slept. There was little furniture of any description in it, excepting a chest or two, and a few dishes for cooking. I was anxious to have our conversation ended, that I might depart. I was another night in one of the old Settler's houses, within a few miles of this. The landlord led me upstairs to see his grain, which he kept on the left. On seeing the quantity, I was surprised that the beams of the house bore the weight of so much wheat, barley and pease, which he had lying there, and for which he could get no sale. Leaving this Settlement, I proceeded to Breadalbane, distant twenty miles. Night overtook me, before I arrived. The road was extremely disagreeable, being through mud and mire, crossing brooks, rivulets, &c. At last it became so dark, and meeting some cross roads, I was at a loss what course to take. As I creeped along I heard a dog barking, apparently at some distance. I was very loath to return, knowing that I would require to strike off the road, and could not discover any bypath. After travelling along through soft mud, I got a little anxious; but falling in with a clearing, I observed a light at some distance, to which I immediately steered, through thick and thin, climbing over logs and fences until I approached it. The house was occupied by a widow and her children. As she had no way of accommodating me herself, she sent one of her boys to direct me to one of her neighbours. After climbing over several windfalls, and sometimes crawling under them, I came to the clearing to which I was directed. I observed the house in the midle of it, steered direct towards the light, and on entering the door, I asked if a stranger would be welcome for a night. They immediately replied, "truly welcome." I sat down and conversed for some time before they knew me. The next morning the landlord took me to see his farm. He had been here for four years, and had about fifteen acres clear, besides three cows and a yoke of oxen, but no sheep. He showed me an elm tree, the circumference of which was fully eighteen feet, the height of it was immense, and it was well proportioned.

After visiting a number of acquaintances in this Settlement, I proceeded towards the Grand River, with the intention of visiting some friends in Lower Canada. I crossed the river at the Long Rapid, and after passing a few days with my friends there, I sailed across the Lake of the two Mountains in a log canoe, and proceeded down the lake side, until I came to the Travace du Roy, or King's Ferry, where I crossed the river the third time. Here I travelled down by the side of Lake St. Louis, where I had much difficulty to procure accommodations, not being acquainted with the French Language. I asked of one the road to Montreal: He replied, "Good road Montreal," which was all the information I could procure from him. Being persuaded that I was on the right road, I travelled on, and after three days arrived at Montreal.

On entering the town, I met a funeral, conducted according to the Roman Catholic form. The whole company consisted of Frenchmen. One half of them were boys of about twelve years of age, all nearly equal in size. They all wore short gowns of white cotton, with black petticoats, stockings, and caps; and marched two in abreast, like a company of trained soldiers. One of the foremost held a cup, apparently silver, in his hand; the other carried the cross. Each of the others carried a candle in his hand. The corpse was in the middle of the rank, and those more advanced in age behind it, decently dressed in black clothes. The Priest marched close to the coffin, constantly reading something out of a French book.

On entering the chapel, the coffin was laid on a table, and all the candles lighted and placed in a circle round it. The Priest read for the space of ten minutes, and then proceeded to the church-yard. I was in the chapel, and observed the people coming in, and dipping their fingers in a bason of water, and crossing their forehead, and then kneeling to pray. The image of the Virgin Mary stood in the farthest end of the chapel, to which the deluded creatures kneeled, when passing it. I stood next to the door, in case I should be requested to retire; but no one molested me, and I retired after the ceremony was finished.

The steam-boat being ready to set off at 10 o'clock at night, I embarked, and paid two dollars for my passage to Quebec, a distance of 180 miles, which we sailed in 24 hours.

Journey from Quebec, to Fredericton.

On the 6th of September, I left Quebec, and crossed the river to Point Levè. On the north side of the river, I enjoyed a most delightful prospect, from a variety of objects; such as, Cape Diamond rising majestically from the river, with the houses along its base, a confused cluster of buildings, overtopping each other, contiguous to the side of the hill; and the awful and terrific Fort, which crowns the Cape. Travelling down the river side, I felt the loss of not being acquainted with the French Language, meeting with no one who could give me the least information or direction but in French. I was aware that I had to leave the St. Lawrence, and cross to Lake Tammisquatta, but when or where I knew not, nor could I find any one that could inform me; until

I happily met with an Englishman, who, though ignorant of the way himself, was acquainted with the French language, and could make inquiry. We soon met a Frenchman, who informed us that the place where I intended to leave the St. Lawrence, for Tammisquatta, was thirty-two leagues from us; and that a village, named Kammoraskau, was just on the point where I should turn from the river. Released with this information, I departed, expressing my gratitude to both my guides, for their kindness. But considering that I had yet to travel about a hundred miles before I left the St. Lawrence, according to the account just now given, I felt some uneasiness at the thought of travelling that distance, among those whose language I did not understand. In about an hour after this, I met with a Frenchman, and, by signs with my fingers, I asked him how far I was from Kammoraskau: he replied, in broken English, fifteen leagues. I thought with myself that I walked amazingly quick, if I had travelled seventeen leagues in an hour. A few hours after this, I observed an old gentleman sitting in a chair before his door. I asked him if he could speak English; he replied, "No English;" but being anxious to ascertain the distance to the above-mentioned village, I approached nearer him, and by signs learned from him that I was about thirty leagues from it. I thanked the old gentleman, and marched on, considering that although the information was disagreeable, yet it agreed with what the first informed me. About five o'clock in the afternoon, I met with another old gentleman, who had not a single word of English. I asked him, by signs, if I could travel to Kammoraskau that night, pointing my finger first to myself, then to Kammoraskau, then to the sun, and to the distant hills under the horizon. He understood at once what I meant, and said, "Hue, hue;" which I interpreted to be, Yes, yes. I walked on pretty quick, flattering myself with the hope of being in Kammoraskau that night. Meeting with a blacksmith, who was an Irishman, I stepped into his shop, and sitting down, I gave him a relation of my misfortunes. He asked me if I understood French. I told him I did not. "I pity you," says he; "I do not know how you get along." I told him that I enquired my way, by means of signs, from those that met me. Then I asked him if I could reach Kammoraskau that night. "If," said he, "you arrive there two days after this, you may think yourself very well off." I then relinquished the hope of getting there that night. I marched on, through a beautiful Settlement, until after sun-set; and passing through the village of St. Thomas, I arrived at a small tavern. The landlord was standing at the door. I asked him if a stranger could be accommodated in his house. He made no reply. I then placed my hand under my head, laying it to one side, and shutting my eyes, showing, as well as I could, what was my object. "O hue, hue," said he, turning in to the house. I followed him, very grateful for the accommodation. He treated me with great civility, but very little conversation of any kind passed between us, during the evening. At bedtime, he signified to me that my bed was ready.

Early the next morning, after having settled with my landlord, I started again to my journey. This day being excessively dry and warm in the forenoon, I walked pretty smart till nine o'clock, and then I went into a tavern to get refreshment. In the afternoon, it rained very heavy, and the soil being of a clayey nature, travelling was very disagreeable. I went into a farmer's house, and sat down. The inmates seemed dejected and destitute. They had nothing to say, though it was much the same to me whether they spoke or not. Not knowing whether or not I was welcome, I determined to rest myself until the rain was over, unless they made signs to me to withdraw. Fortunately the day cleared up in a little. I bade the silent family farewell, but they returned no answer. It was then drawing towards evening, and I deemed it prudent to provide lodgings before very late, as I was in a strange country. I resolved to ask the first person I met, how far I was from the first tavern, but how to accomplish my purpose by signs was the next consideration. I called at the first house I observed, and asked the distance in English. They replied in French, but what was said I knew not. Then I pointed my finger as if it were in a straight direction before me on the road; then put my thumb and forefinger to my mouth, turning up the little finger, as if I was drinking a glass. I could not make them understand what I meant, and after continuing for some time making signs, as well as I could, and they on the other hand replying, we had to part as ignorant as when we met.

I met with several individuals on the way, but could learn nothing from them to relieve my anxiety. At last night coming on, I was determined to go into the first house I met with, and ask the favour of allowing me to sit by the fire-side till day-light. Accordingly, I called, and by signs, as before, inquired for a tavern. They replied, "No, no," which was all the English I heard from them. Probably they supposed that I was asking if it was a public-house. However they made signs to me to sit down, and I complied thankfully. They all crowded round the fire, and carried on their own diversion. I drew aside to a corner, that they might have more room. Occasionally, in the midst of their mirth, they fixed their eyes on me, and laughed heartily. Whether I was the object of their mirth or not, I knew not; but I studied to give them as little occasion as possible. I did not feel myself happy with them. At supper-time, they dropped their play and merriment, and asked me to sit at table, and take a share along with the rest. Supper being ended, they retired to one side of the house, singly, or in pairs, as they thought proper, to perform noted exercises of Roman Catholic worship, which they called their duty, such as crossing their breasts, counting beads, &c. During the time they attended to these forms, if their assistance was necessary through the house, they could leave them off, and, when it was finished, resume their devotional exercises. I was then directed to a bed in a corner of the house, without a single sheet or blanket, consisting only of a wretched tyke, from the seams of which the straw jutted out, and rendered my situation very disagreeable. I took off my shoes, and, placing my bundle under my head for a pillow, I slept more comfortably than I expected.

Next morning I started at day-light, and asked what was to pay. I received some answer, but I understood it not. I then gave the landlord a shilling. From his examining it, I conjectured he thought it was either too much or too little: I then offered him a quarter of a dollar, (one and threepence), but instantly he made a bow, repeating "c'est bon," which convinced me that he was satisfied, and then we parted.

This day I met on the road a handsome young couple, who had left the Province of New-Brunswick, and were bound for Upper Canada. I thought, from their familiarity, and their own confession, that they were married; but I learned afterwards that they were the off-spring of the same father, but of different mothers. I overtook two Irishmen, with their wives and two infants, who had lately arrived at Quebec, and were bound for St. John's, New-Brunswick, a distance of more than 400 miles. The two men carried their bedding upon their backs, and the women the children, and some kettles to cook their victuals, which formed all their baggage. I asked them what was their intention in going such a contrary route. They informed me that some of their relations, residing near St. John's, had sent for them, and that they could find no passage more convenient than by Quebec. "But," said they, "we thought, while in Ireland, if we only landed any where on the other side of the Atlantic, that we would be then in the land of promise, and could soon find out our relations." After giving them all the information I could concerning their route, I left them. I tried to persuade them to give up their journey, considering how far the season was advanced, as I was aware of the difficulties they had to encounter, by reason of lakes, rivers, forests, &c. but they were so anxious to see their relations, that they would not listen to my advice.

After travelling for three days successively, from day-light till night, I arrived at the foot of the carrying-place, fifteen miles below Kammoraskau, where I intended to leave the river St. Lawrence.

On Sunday evening, just as I was going to bed, in an inferior tavern, a number of the neighbouring youngsters collected to drink; and, being well advanced, some of the females began to sing, and the rest to dance. I was lulled asleep with their mirth, but had not continued long so when they awakened me, bringing liquor with them, and compelling me to take it. After complying with their pressing invitation, I knew by their countenance and motions that they were well pleased. The whole of them crowded to see such a phenomenon. They continued dancing until they were exhausted, and then retired. Next morning, being the 10th September, I left the St. Lawrence, and ascended a height on the south side of the river, where I met with a kind of road, cut through the woods, to another Settlement about six miles from the river. Here I met with an old Indian, who informed me that he was going to the tavern I just left, for a bottle of rum he was to take with him on his journey to Lake Tammisquatta, being the same route that I was going. I told him I would wait for him, and would be glad of his company, for he spoke pretty good English. There were three other Indians, who were to accompany him, sitting by a fire on the road side, where they had passed the night. They were cooking breakfast, while their companion went for the rum. I hurried on to the next Settlement to get breakfast, in order to be ready to go with them. Getting refreshment, I rested until they came. Happily I met an old lady, (the wife of a disbanded soldier), who informed me that I must lodge in the solitary desert all night if I should proceed on my journey so late in the day. The Indians in the mean time approached us, struck fire, and cooked dinner. One of them, as soon as he had dined, took up the canoe and marched; the rest smoking their pipes. The old Indian that went for the rum made rather free with it before he overtook the rest, which rendered him unable to take his turn of the canoe. However, his companions being stout and nimble, they carried it by turns, and walked amazingly expeditious. Taking the advice of the old lady, I staid till next morning, thinking it would not be difficult to overtake them the next day.

Getting up early, I set off, having to travel thirty miles before I would meet a single house. The road was exceedingly disagreeable, sometimes through soft swamps, and sometimes over hills, rocks, and mountains, which made travelling very fatiguing. I observed by the road side vestiges of fire not wholly extinguished, and I concluded that the Indians took up their abode by it all night, and could not be very far before me. I travelled with a quick pace, being anxious to overtake them, as I was informed that there was no possibility in getting a passage, when I came to the lake. excepting in some of their canoes. In the afternoon I discovered marks of another fire, where I supposed they had cooked dinner; but I thought certainly that they could not be those whom I had seen, otherwise I must have overtaken them before now, as their canoe was of a considerable bulk and weight. In a little I met with three Irishmen, carrying their baggage, who had left the city of St. John's, and bound for Upper Canada. They told me of the distance the Indians were before me, but I understood they were not the same party to whom I had been speaking for a passage the day before. After having ended my conversation with the Irishmen, I pushed on to overtake the Indians, in order, if possible, to procure a passage in their canoe. About four in the afternoon I overtook them, consisting only of a young couple and a boy of sixteen years of age. Their baggage consisted of a small canoe, a small hatchet, a tin kettle, and a few herrings. I was desirous to have a conversation with them, chiefly for my own interest, but they seemed very distant and indifferent. Being unacquainted with their manner of carrying the canoe, and yet anxious to do them any service in my power, I carried the *tommahawk.** The two men alternately carried the canoe; having a cross belt on the crown of their head, on which the canoe was supported; one of the cross pieces resting on a piece of board which hung down their back. The canoe was bottom upwards, with the one end stretching forward over their heads, and the other sometimes touching the ground. When they got it in order on their back they could travel pretty quick, but changing so often caused a delay, and obstructed our progress. The day being now far spent, I was doubtful if I could make out the lake that night. I marched on and left them. But after I travelled some distance, I reflected that it would not answer to take the hatchet with me if the Indians were to camp on the way that night, for they could not conveniently want it. Being at a loss what to do, whether to return with the hatchet or to proceed on my march, I rested myself to deliberate on the step I should take, thinking perhaps they would make their appearance before I removed. I knew they had but little or no provisions to themselves, and to deprive them of the hatchet, which they could not

*A small hatchet

well want, was what I was reluctant to do. While I was sitting, I fortunately saw some pheasants close by; aiming at one of them with a stone, I killed it. As the Indians had fire-works, I thought I could get it roasted for supper, and that it was providentially brought in my way. But after staying here a long time, and no appearance of the party coming, I got very uneasy, and was at a loss what to do. At last I thought, in case how I might be used by the Indians, that I had better proceed. The night being warm and dry, and having the pheasant, I saw I could not be ill off, on the supposition I had to pass the night in a bush, even if I had to eat my venison raw. Being yet day-light, I marched on, and in a little while I ascended a height from which I could discern the lake, though at a distance. My joy was more easily conceived than expressed. I walked with expedition and vigour, thinking to reach it before night. Having descended the hill, my march was through a low and level tract, which made it appear to be nearer night than it was. After travelling some miles through this low place, I again became discouraged, supposing I had only seen the blue sky instead of the lake; but the next height happily removed my doubts. In a little I came to a small house on the border of the lake. When I was just done with supper, the Indians arrived with their canoe. They pretended to be making preparations for embarking that same night. Seeing this, I enquired of my landlord if there was any possibility of getting a passage any other way than with them. He told me there was very little chance, without paying more than I could afford. So I applied immediately to them in order to procure a passage to the next Settlement, which was forty-five miles distant. I asked them what they would take for conveying me that distance; but they would not come to any agreement unless I paid them so much per advance. They told me they intended to encamp by the lake-side all night, and they had nothing to eat, excepting a few herrings which they brought from the St. Lawrence; and these were a little injured in consequence of being carried in a bundle on the back of the squaw; the heat rendering their taste disagreeable. Here I was put to a stand what to do, suspecting if I was to pay them beforehand they might set off early in the morning and leave me behind. I told them I was afraid of this. They promised faithfully not to deceive me. Being however doubtful of them, I gave them only a quarter of a dollar to buy some flour for supper. I then returned to the house and fetched the pheasant which I had killed; but when I came back, I could neither see Indians, canoe, or any thing else. Apprehensive of being disappointed in my expectation, I cried out. They made answer, having retired a little from the place where I left them to a more convenient station. I presented the pheasant to them, for which they were very thankful, and then returned to my lodgings. The landlord was an American, and could speak English with propriety. The landlady was a French woman from Lower Canada, and consequently all the family spoke the French language. After having some conversation with the old gentleman I retired to bed. I got up early next morning. Indeed I slept very little all night, fearing I might be deceived by the treacherous Indians. I dressed myself with all expedition, being determined to put off no time till I knew whether they had gone or not. When I came to the place I found the sunap and the squaw on one side of the fire, with a rag of a blanket under them, and another above them. The boy was opposite on the other side of the fire, rolled in an old tattered blanket. The three were fast asleep. The canoe was turned bottom upwards, and the few articles that formed their baggage secured under it. I awakened them, and enquired when they intended to set off. They said immediately after breakfast. The squaw getting up began to cook. The sunap fixed two small stakes in the ground, with another across, on which the kettle was hung. The squaw had a quantity of flour, of which she made porridge, cutting the unsavoury herrings, and mixing them with the porridge. While she was employed cooking, other considerations occupied my attention. I thought if I would return to breakfast, they might set off before I could return. To fast till we got to the next Settlement would be dangerous, and to partake with the Indians I felt no inclination; on the supposition I would be made welcome. I remained until I saw the porridge ready. It was poured into a platter made of bark. Each of them had an Indian spoon, also made of bark. They offered me one, and requested me to partake with them. Considering the distance before me, and at the same time fearing I should disoblige them by refusing, rather than from any immediate want, I complied. We all four sat round the platter, thankful that we were not worse. The diet was a rarity to me, and I believe would be so to any European. After breakfast one of them made a paddle for me to help them. All things being prepared we set off. One of the Indians was in the bow of the canoe, and the other in the stern. I sat next to the latter, paddling away, and the squaw sat next to the former, smoking her pipe. My companion in the stern soon broke his paddle, which relieved me very agreeably from my labour, and afterwards I was only a spectator of what was going on.

Towards the middle of the day, it began to rain, and we came ashore to shelter ourselves. Any baggage we had was kept dry under the canoe. The squaw staid beside it while we retired under some bushes until it got fair. Here I had my suspicions that they might leave me in the midst of a wilderness, from which I had no prospect ever to come out alive; or that they might, for the sake of any little things I possessed, be tempted to take my life. Could I at this time have had an opportunity of conversing with my friends, I would have earnestly persuaded them to content themselves in their native country, however indifferent their circumstances might be. My suspicions were without foundation, and betrayed a heart, perhaps, more treacherous than that of the poor Indians, who never offered to do me the least injury. The day cleared up, and we re-embarked, but in a little time it rained again very heavy, and as we were on the middle of the lake, we could not conveniently come ashore, and the rain penetrated to our skin. We paddled away in this condition, till we reached the end of the lake, for the wind was rising; and as the canoe was very small, and rather heavy loaded, with so many in it, fear of consequences, made us to overlook what we suffered from the rain. However, in a short time, we gained the end of the lake, and then had a fine calm, and swift current, down the river. The day was far advanced, and though we had an appetite for dinner, we had no provisions, and there was no house within fifteen miles of us. We did not know how far we were from the next house at that time, and the expectation of reaching it supported our spirits. Our hunger at last became insufferable. The squaw found two cold potatoes amongst her rags, in the bottom of the canoe: she gave one of them to her sunap, and ate the other herself, which caused the boy and I to feel more keenly than if we had not seen them. Our spirits were revived by the sight of a canoe, at a distance, polling up towards us. this afforded more joy than we could easily express, although we were uncertain whether we could find any provisions in it. My companions, however, were in good hope, as they perceived it to be an Indian canoe. On approaching it nearer, we discovered an old Indian sitting in the bow, and his daughter, polling along with amazing rapidity against the current. We asked them if they had any spare provisions. The old man replied, that they had nothing but a small bit of raw pork, which, hungry as we were, we could not relish. They informed us that the next Settlement was at least eight miles from us, which discouraged us more than if we had not met them. The young Indian, impatient and anxious to get along, paddled so hard, that he broke his paddle the second time. I perceived by the countenance of the old Indian, that he was much displeased, as he had to steer to the shore to make another one, which interrupted us considerably. When done, we set off, and in a little, we discovered a small cottage, bordering on the river. I called there, and bought a few potaoes to my companions, which they boiled with great haste, and having a few herrings, they partook of the mess with great cheerfulness. I got some bread and milk to myself, which formed one of the most palatable meals I ever took. After this repast, we proceeded, and arrived late at the next Settlement. As we approached the first house on the river side, we heard the murmur, as of a waterfall, right before us. The two Indians both stood up in the canoe, setting their paddles against the rocks and stones to keep the canoe at leisure, as the current ran quite rapid. The squaw, terrified, took hold of the two gunwales, repeating something which expressed her alarm. Her sunap turned round and spoke, apparently requesting her to be quiet. The noise of the falls rendered me a little uneasy, being close to them, and could not get ashore until we went farther down the face of the rock. However, I thought they did not intend to drown the squaw, at any rate; and that, at all events, unless Providence determined otherwise, I could extricate myself, in case of extreme danger, better than she could. My anxiety, however, was in a little relieved by the prospect of a landing-place just at the edge of the falls. Here we hauled our canoe ashore, carried it up to the house, which was not far off, and stepped in, not knowing whether welcome or not. The people were remarkably civil, and as they had accommodations for travellers, they entertained us very kindly. Need I mention how comfortably I felt myself before a good fire, with a plentiful supply of agreeable provisions. After supper, the landlady made me a bed right before the fire. The sunap and his squaw were accommodated on one side of it, and the boy on the other. The landlord and landlady retired to a kind of a bed in one of the farthest corners of the house; and the two sons lay on the floor in the other corner, with the skin of a buffalo below them, and another above them. The daughter slept also on the floor, at the foot of her parents' bed, with a couple of old thread-bare blankets rolled about her.

We got up early next morning, and by means of the Indian, I understood from our landlady what was to pay, and after settling with her, we departed. We carried the canoe to the river side below the falls, and just as I was stepping in, the Indian informed me that he would take me no farther, until he knew what allowance I was to give him. I agreed with him, and requested him to land me on the opposite side of the Madawaskau river, where I could travel along on foot. After agreement, we proceeded, but instead of setting me across, as he promised, he took me down some distance upon the same side, and on seeing an Indian wigwam, he and his companions went ashore. They neither requested me to go with them to the wigwam, nor to remain till they would return. Through bogs and brooks, I made my way down the river side, until I met a canoe about ten miles below where I left the Indians. Here I crossed the river, and arrived at a Frenchman's house, possessed by an old lady and her three daughters, none of whom had a word of English. To my great surprise and happiness, I understood in a little, that she was the mother of a young gentleman who accompanied the Surveyor-General, the same year that I was in the exploring party. He soon came into the house, and I knew him perfectly well. By this time he could speak English pretty well, which endeared him to me as a near relation. I staid with him all that day. The next morning I bought a small canoe for a dollar: It had been so long unused, and exposed to the sun, that there were chinks in the bottom, which I filled up with tow. I hauled it into the water, to see how it would do, but being very light, and having no ballast, it overturned, and tumbled me into the river. I then dragged it ashore, put in some stones for ballast, and, lest it should again upset, I tied my bundle to a small line which was made fast in the bow. The Frenchman made me a small paddle, and then I set off. The wind blowing straight down the river, I had very little to do but steer. I made out the Portage about noon, which was twenty-four miles from the place I left in the morning. I paid a quarter of a dollar for dragging the canoe across the Portage, which is three quarters of a mile. I went to visit the falls;* but having previously seen the falls of Niagara, these appeared so trifling that I returned without making any particular observation.

Getting my canoe across, and ballasting it with stones as before, I proceeded. I had great difficulty in getting through the White Rapids: the water being so low, and forming a rapid stream in the middle of the channel, enrolled with foam, formed by the current dashing against the rocks and stones, partly seen, and partly concealed in the channel. The rock on both sides was so steep that it was impossible to get along, except through these rough and boisterous billows. I observed one channel which appeared navigable for my light canoe. I pointed her stern towards it, and though at some distance from it, such was the rapidity of the current, that before I was aware, I was in the middle of it. I endeavoured to steer between two large stones

*The grand Falls of St. John's River.

which were almost level with the surface of the water, and the rapid current rolling over them. The third stone was directly before, not more than the length of the canoe from the former, which I could not possibly avoid, and which I thought would upset the canoe; but from the force with which it was driven, it slid over it without any other damage than injuring the bottom a little, so that it became leaky, but I had no time to remedy that till I fairly passed through the Rapids. I then took my knife and squeezed the tow into the chinks again, and discharged the water that was in her with my shoe. Having then got into fine smooth but rapid water, and while I was examining whether or not the bottom was sufficient, the fore part of the canoe dashed against a large stone, which lay in the middle of the river, about eight inches above the surface of the water. I was sitting in the stern, and when the fore part of the canoe struck upon the stone, by the rapidity of the current, the canoe went up on the top of it. I jumped immediately to the fore part and weighed it down, then I put my foot on the stern to lighten the canoe, and thus extricated myself quite safe. Being fatigued paddling all day through the Rapids, and the night now approaching, having paddled about forty miles, I went ashore, and called at a small hut on the bank of the river, which was full of grain, without any individual near it, and then returned to my canoe, and went ashore nigh a small house, which I found occupied by an old soldier, one of the West India Rangers. He made me heartily welcome to a share of such as he had. A number of the neighbouring soldiers collected in his house, to drink a cag of rum. They had finished reaping the same day.

After leaving the soldier's house, I came to another Settlement, distant ten miles from it. Here I took breakfast, and got some potatoes and salmon, boiled them, and placed them in the fore part of my canoe. I then proceeded paddling down the river.

The wind being favourable, I erected a pine bush in the bow, for a sail; by the assistance of which, it run amazingly swift through the water, while I had only to steer it. When I approached the Meductic Falls, I had to lower my sail, and haul the canoe along the sand-bar, for fear of being drawn into the current. After dragging it for the distance of 100 yards, amongst a number of large stones, the water coming up to the ancle, I got into smooth water again. I then jumped in, set up my former sail, and steered away. Being on water from day-light till dark, I went ashore at a house near the river side. It was occupied by a Frenchman. I signified to him by signs, that I wanted lodgings. He gave me an old quilted rug, and directed me to the barn. A cart-ful of hay stood in the middle of the floor. I ascended to the top of it, prepared, and rolled myself into the quilt, and lay down covered with hay. In a little after, I heard some person coming into the barn, which somewhat startled me, thinking that it was the Frenchman coming to rob me. But the person retired into a corner, and lay down to rest him-self. I concluded he must be some poor traveller like my-self, and my fears being removed, I slept comfortably until day-light. I got up early next morning, left the quilt at the door, and set off in my canoe, and about noon arrived at Fredericton.

Journey from Fredericton to Magegadavick.

Here I tried to sell my canoe, but the people supposing that I had found her adrift, or perhaps stolen her, would not make me an offer. I dragged her ashore, and left her there. I set off, and travelled down the river-side, until I came to the river Oromocto. After taking some refreshment, I left that Settlement. The sun was just below the horizon as I entered the desert, and I had seven miles to travel before I came to the next Settlement. Night coming on, and being wearied with my journey, I began to be very impatient. At last I came to a lonely house, and rapped at the door, but no body answered. I went round it, repeatedly, but could observe no appearance of light. I knocked several times, but all in vain. Much fatigued, and disappointed, I set off, wishing I had staid in the last Settlement. After I had travelled for some time upon a narrow cut road in the middle of a wilderness, at last I came to a clearing, where I discovered a light at some distance. Encouraged, I hastened my pace, and on arriving, found the house from which the light shined, occupied by an old lady and her two daughters. My application for lodgings was immediately granted. Taking some refreshment, I went to bed, grateful for the accommodation which kind Providence prepared me.

Early next day, being the 19th of September, I set off for Magegadavick River. The morning was clear and cold; the ground being covered with hoar-frost. I had to travel nine miles before I could get breakfast, but I was not the least intimidated, as I found myself amongst people of whom I could ask whatever I wanted. After breakfast, I crossed the Oromocto again; travelled through the desert, until I came to a small house possessed by a soldier. It being at this time past mid-day, I asked if I could get any refreshment. They replied they had only a handful of flour, on which they depended for sustenace, until they went to Fredericton, and they could not give me any share of it. I directed my way then for Magegadavick, which was thirteen miles off, at which I arrived faint and fatigued, before it was dark. Here I was comfortably accommodated with victuals and lodging.

Early next morning, I started for the mouth of the river, travelled seventeen miles down the river-side, through a thick forest, and by the middle of the day, arrived at the Settlement, from which I proceeded. In a little, I had a happy meeting with relations and acquaintances. Calculating the distance I had travelled in my last tour, I ascertained it to be *One thousand nine hundred and seventy miles.*

After having staid here a few months, I thought of returning to my native country; and finding a small Brig loading in Degidequash, bound for Greenock, I applied to the Captain for a passage; but the vessel being but small, and having her full complement of men, he would not condescend to accept of my application. The Brig being old and leaky, I felt somewhat indifferent at meeting with a refusal. Afterwards I was informed that she was wrecked on the Western Isles of Scotland. Hearing this, I was convinced that Divine Providence, for my good, had counteracted my intention of sailing in her. However, I did not drop the idea of visiting Scotland, though I contented myself to spend that winter in New-Brunswick, as it was too late in the season to cross the Atlantic. After passing the seventh winter in this cold woodland country, I determined, if possible, to leave it in the following summer.

Voyage from St. Andrew's to Greenock.

In the month of June, 1823, I went on board the Marion of Greenock, bound for that place, with a load of timber. The Captain and one of the sailors, together with three hands which were employed in loading the vessel, were all unfortunately drowned, a few days before we departed. Besides these, there were three other hands, belonging to the vessel, made off, while she was a-loading, which reduced five of her usual complement. The first Mate had the charge of the ship; who, after making every attempt to employ hands, was under the necessity of taking up two drunken sailors, whom he found on the streets, belonging to some of the ships lying in the harbour. While we were employed in taking out their hammocks at a back window, one of them was seized by a constable, and taken from us. Having got his companion into the boat, we rowed off to the ship, concealing him under the seats, for fear of being discovered by his master, whose vessel was close to our's. We immediately observed the jolly-boat of that vessel making ready, and steering direct to our ship; but, happily, we got the man put into the cabin, just as they were climbing up the other side of our vessel. Whether they had any suspicion of what was done, I know not; but, staying on board awhile, they retired, without further search.

June the 6th, we weighed anchor, and set sail. It was so calm that the strength of the tide almost drove us upon a rocky point on Campbell's Island; however, we soon got her out in the middle by towing.

In the afternoon, the wind blew up from the southward, which was straight a-head. We steered to harbour near West Quady Light-house, where we anchored all night. Next morning, four hands were sent with the jolly-boat, to send the Pilot ashore. One of these, being the same that was stolen from the other ship, immediately on his landing, made his escape through the woods. They returned directly with the boat, and apprised us of what had happened; but it was in vain to go in search of him. We went ashore to Lieubec, for the purpose of getting more hands; but could get none upon any conditions. While on shore, it thundered dreadfully, and the rain penetrated to our very skin, before we got on board. A council was then held, respecting the management of the ship. The sailors wished to return to St. Andrew's for hands, but the Master flattering them by promising some extra grog and wages, they at last agreed to set off with the number we had, saying, "We are few, but true-hearted."

We had to go ashore for help to weigh anchor; and the wind blew so tremendously, that we were baffled in our first attempt to regain the vessel. Making a second attempt, with difficulty we succeeded, being wet to the skin with the spray. After much labour we got up the anchor, hoisted sail, and set off with a fair breeze. In the evening the wind ceased, and it was so calm, that we made little progress during the night.

The next morning, being sunday, we steered S. E. and made out Cape Sables towards evening, and lost sight of land that same night. At twelve o'clock at night, a tremendous gale blew. All hands were called upon deck, to rief topsails. The sailors, while speedily putting on their clothes, were cursing and swearing shockingly. The top-gallant sails were immediately furled, and a double rief taken in the top-sails; she then rightened a little. The watch were then permitted to go to bed, but in a little they were called again to take off the foresail. For my part, I could do little service at this time, being affected with sea-sickness. The ship heeled over so, that we could scarcely stand on deck. She was dashed and driven away at a terrible rate. The froth she hove from her bow passed the side, appearing like a stream of fire. In consequence of the excessive darkness of the night, we could not see the length of the vessel. Nothing appeared to our view but a raging sea, appearing like columns of fire beneath, and darkness above; a tremendous gale blowing; rain pouring on in torrents; our clothes on our backs dripping; and heavy sails, at the same time, to furl; while we were five hands short, with a leaky ship, and the pumps making water fast. All hands, excepting the one at the helm, went to furl the foresail. With great difficulty, we got it and every stitch furled excepting the main-sail, which was close riefed. After that, we hove her to, being the last shift. While in this consternation daylight appeared, but brought no relief. Nothing was seen but a sea rising with billows. It broke in torrents over the bow; but not mountain high, (as some would say), which left us sometimes up to the thigh in water, upon the lee-side. You would think the spray by its dashing, threatened to drive the cook-house over-board. All hands went below, excepting the helms-man, each cursing his own eyes if ever he saw such a storm as this. I was then brought to a heart-rent conviction of my forwardness in coming to sea, after having been previously so providentially and wonderfully preserved from the foaming ocean. Now I thought was the period in which I behoved to launch into the invisible world, prepared or not prepared. I stood upon the windward-side grasping the rail in my hand. Every wave and motion of the vessel added to my terror. I wished I were ashore, though it were but on a rock, on which I might have the breadth of the soles of my feet, and have the comfort of dying by degrees. I had but little or no hopes of ever seeing land. This consideration excited the following reflections: Is it true that I am in this condition, or do I dream; but, alas! twenty, thirty long hours is too long to dream. What have I done? I came to sea against the advice of all my relations. Twice I attempted to come before, and was prevented by Divine Providence. This is the third time, and I am permitted to throw myself into this awful condition. Well might I compare myself to the fig-tree, respecting which the gardener prayed to save this year also. It added much to my grief, to think that I was so wonderfully preserved not only for one year, but for nearly five years, and yet having very little appearance of any fruit. The Lord, however, in his kind Providence, and for purposes known to himself spared me whole. About five o'clock the next morning, the wind abated to a pleasant breeze, so as to enable us to hoist all sails—the sailors repeating, "Huzza, my boys, for the land of cakes!" all apparently forgetful of the danger that had threatened them.

The wind continued still to blow from the northward, so that we were driven to the fortieth degree of North latitude. We had then a pleasant gale from the S. W. which continued for several days, in which time we espied several vessels at a distance. We spoke two Yankee ships, the one bound for Amsterdam, and the other for Philadelphia, from some port in Russia, with passengers, having been sixty-one days out, and was only about half way across the Atlantic.

The wind continued blowing from the west for seven days, when it came round again to the northward, and drove us the second time to the southward, where we got becalmed for twenty-four hours. We then aimed for Cape Clear and the Irish Channel, but suddenly a southerly wind sprung up, and we made straight for the North Channel. the wind came round to S. W. and from that to W. S. W. A little after dark, it blew very strong, accompanied with heavy rain, which continued all night. Fortunately it blew uniformly, so that we had nothing to do but look on. The vessel sailed at the rate of seven knots an hour, which was more than she did at any other period during the passage. I sat down beside the bulwarks, shoved my head in under a piece of a spare sail, lying on the quarter deck, having no other shelter from the rain, which still continued pouring on in torrents. Bad as my shelter was, I was soon called to a worse. The man at the helm ordered to ring the four bells; when I had to take my turn, which I was obliged to do, as there were only other two in our watch that took the helm, whereas there should be seven in each watch. I now thought how foolish I was thus to expose myself to such fatigue and danger, merely for the prospect of having an interview with my relations, and of seeing my country. My clothes were as wet as if taken out of the water, and I had not even so much time as to wring my jacket. The wind blew right aft, and the night was so dark that it was impossible to discern the bow of the vessel, or to watch her motions. After our four hours were expired, we were permitted to turn in for other four, leaving our wet clothes on the top of our chests, till we were called again; when we were under the necessity of putting them on, wet as they were; which was certainly sufficient to affect the strongest constitution.

This wet and blowing weather continued during the remainder of the voyage, which exhausted us very much, being so few in number, and obliged to keep constantly pumping.

One day, as I was walking on deck, meeting our aged cook, he asked me, how soon the master expected to reach land. I told him, In three days, if the wind continues, he expects to make Tory Island. "O well," says the poor old man with joy; "and after that the Rachries, and the Mull of Kintyre, and then the Clough." Yes, said I, and then Gourock, and a happy meeting with the wife. "Oh sir!" exclaimed the poor old man, shrugging his shoulders, and shedding tears of joy.

The morning we expected to see the land, we espied a small sloop at break of day. We immediately made towards her, but she, steering almost the same course with us, we made but little progress towards her. The master ordered to make more sail, saying, "Let us approach her, in the name of our Creator, to ascertain where we are." We immediately obeyed, and soon made up to the other vessel. We asked what was the nearest land. "Aranmore," replied they. "What course?" The Captain, not hearing any answer, asked a second time; which was answered, "Aranmore!" Fearing our vessel would strike them, they kept at a distance; and we steered for land.

Our watch turned in, and at eight o'clock in the morning, putting my head out at the cabin door, I observed something green on each side. I rubbed my eyes, being somewhat drowsy, when I plainly discovered the hills, houses, and rows of Irish potatoes on Tory Island one of the most joyful sights I have ever seen.

The wind being right aft, and blowing fresh along the coast of Ireland, rendered it requisite that two hands should attend the helm, who had to stand almost the four hours without relief. The rest of the crew were kept constantly pumping, every other hour, by which we were almost spent out. A sight of the Western Isles of Scotland, however, cheered our hearts; and by 11 o'clock at night, we passed the Mull of Kintyre. Being my turn at the helm, I was so overjoyed on entering the Clyde, that I paid little regard to the time, so that I allowed the glass to run out, and knew not how long, which kept our watch longer out than it ought. For this fault I deserved to be laid across the windlass, but as I was a raw seaman, and had permitted the other watch to sleep an hour longer, I was freely pardoned. At 8 o'clock next morning the Pilot came on board; and, having a light breeze, at 10 o'clock, we dropped anchor close to Greenock.

After having secured the sails, and pumped the water out of the vessel, we went ashore. The sailors' wives, with their children in their arms, stood on the quay, welcoming their husbands. But how disappointed was the Captain's wife, who, instead of meeting with him, only received the remains of his clothes! His body was so swelled with the water, that his coat could not be taken off without tearing it. In a short time, the sailors were jumping and roaring about the streets, crying, "Call the watch, hold the reel," &c. But by the afternoon, the most of them were so overcome with liquor and sleep, that they knew not where they had laid down their heads, till next morning.

On the 8th of July, I took the steam-boat to Glasgow, and from thence proceeded towards my former place of residence, flattering myself with the hope of attaining happiness, so soon as I arrived: But alas! to my great disappointment, I found that, if it ever was there, it had vanished away, "as the morning cloud, and as the early dew."

Andrew Young, Printer, 150, Trongate.

This is Number

878

of a limited edition
of 1000 copies

Printed in Canada by
Centennial Print & Litho Ltd.
and bound by
R. & R. Bookbinding
Fredericton, New Brunswick, Canada